Born and raised ... ... nds, Toby Campion is a UK National Poetry Slam Champion and a World Poetry Slam finalist. Recipient of the Silver Wyvern Award and First Place in the Poetry on the Lake Prizes 2017, awarded by Carol Ann Duffy, Toby has performed his poetry on stages across the UK, from Glastonbury Festival to London's Royal Albert Hall, and in countries around the world, including America, Italy, Spain, Albania and South Korea. His debut play, WRECK, won the Fifth Word Theatre Award for Most Promising Playwright 2015.

Toby's poetry has been selected to represent the UK at numerous international conferences and events including Capturing Fire: International Queer Poetry Summit, the 18th Biennale of Young Artists from Europe and the Mediterranean, the Paris Poetry World Cup and Next Generation Speaks. Director of UniSlam and Resident Artist at Camden's prestigious Roundhouse, Toby was one of the first resident poets of the River Thames.

Through your blood

Toby Campion

Burning Eye

BurningEyeBooks
Never Knowingly
Mainstream

This edition published by Burning Eye Books 2017

www.burningeye.co.uk

@burningeyebooks

Burning Eye Books
15 West Hill, Portishead, BS20 6LG

ISBN 978 1 911570 12 7

Through your blood

CONTENTS

GRANDPA TERRY	11
OLD FRIEND	12
NITS	14
LEARNING TO HOLD	16
LION'S PRIDE	18
SUMMERTIME STRETCH	20
WHEN SOMEONE HAS DROWNED	22
LEARNING TO SWALLOW	23
IATROGENIC	24
TELLING THE LADS	25
DELIVERANCE	26
LANDSLIDE IN THE CHESTERFIELD AREA	30
'MAKE LEICESTER *BRITISH*'	31
LANDSLIDE IN THE CHESTERFIELD AREA	33
FROM THE MIDLANDS	34
WHEN THE STRANGER CALLED ME A FAGGOT	36
LANDSLIDE IN THE CHESTERFIELD AREA	37
WHEN I SEE	38
LEARNING TO DRIVE	42
SUMMER JOB LIFEGUARDING ON LAKE FISHKILL	44
NOTES FROM MYKONOS BEACH AT 3AM	45
NOTES FROM THE AIRPORT BAR, A WEEK LATER, INTOXICATED	46
NOTES FROM THE SEXUAL HEALTH CLINIC WAITING ROOM	48

SAMARITAN   50

GRAVE   51

WHEN YOU HOLD SOMETHING IN   52

THE BOY WHO PRAYED   53

LEARNING TO DANCE   56

ACCORDING TO THE BOOK OF SAMUEL   60

Warn us of becoming our fathers,
who were taught to become their fathers,
who were taught to ration softness
like dried fruit,
to stash their shadows
below floorboards,
who were taught to fight
as if tears were the enemy,
the same battle which fills
the trenches between
our inherited ribs.

> Mother in thy mercy,
> hear our prayer.

GRANDPA TERRY

Grandpa Terry lets me stamp on his beer cans
before he throws them out. They crunch
into metal mince pies and I tell him
to drink quicker so I can jump on more.

My sister performs a dance routine for him
– *Say You'll Be There* by the Spice Girls –
and his cheeks are streams of tinsel.
The only boy of ten grandchildren,

I have perfected my surprised face
when unwrapping Superman merchandise.
My mum and dad give me the only present
I asked for: Winter Sports Barbie.

She comes drenched in a skin-tight glitter
bodysuit and her hair is a crimped blizzard.
She looks how I imagine my dreams would look
if I stuck their feet to a pink snowboard

and asked them to lose weight. I call her Angela.
Grandpa Terry watches from the back door
as Angela glides across the frozen lake
of my nan's birdbath. She sings *Say You'll Be There*

and skis through the air on her hands.
Behind me, I feel Grandpa Terry's lips plié
open and closed, like my older cousins' do
whenever I mention Santa.

Wanting to say something, thinking better of it.
Avalanche stopping just short of the village.
Grandpa Terry crushes something below his sigh,
turns his back, leaves me

an empty beer can in the snow.

OLD FRIEND

I would say I love what you've both done
with the house but the wallpaper is horrible.
And it's difficult to appreciate someone's furniture
properly when you're hiding in their back garden.
Am I a tree? Am I a bush?
No, I'm a psychopath.
You are cooking lamb.

Your wife is frustratingly beautiful.
The silk of her dress flows so effortlessly
over all I couldn't give: her hips,
the possibility they bear.
Christmases with your parents are peaceful.
Dinner is not served with snide remarks or silence,
your father's shame spoiling the gravy.

You hold her hand when you leave the house
and the topic of your marriage does not earn rental
in the mouths of neighbours, or legislators.
I see crayon-stained sofas, crisps crushed
into carpets; you have three annoying children.
And you are a brilliant dad,
as I knew you would be.

No need to pack armour into lunchboxes,
they are not forced to defend you in the playground,
to bite down the trembling loyalty of their bottom lips,
dignified indignity. Their eyes are as wide
and oblivious as they should be.
And I tell myself things are better off like this.
But I can't help wondering.

You tell your children you love them unconditionally,
and I wonder how things would have been
if you were able to tell yourself that.

You tell your wife *forever*.
I wonder, has she ever tasted
the salt of my name on your lips before?

Does she know what it means to die in someone's mouth?
Did she lick your teeth clean of me
or is some of my bitter still stuck in your cavities,

between the fractures below your heavy cheeks?
I hear your bones crack in my sleep.
I wonder if you hear mine,

do you dream?
Have you kept me
hidden somewhere
in this fine house you have built yourself into?
At the back of the drinks cabinet
or the sock drawer?
The patch of ceiling above the bed?
Am I the lamb on your table,
something you have carved? A sacrifice
under the hunger for the flat-pack ease
of all this?

NITS

As a child I don't know how many times
I got nits. My mum would drag me
to the bathroom, maybe twice a month
in peak season.

Oh God, how has this happened again?

Out came the white comb, twelve-minute
head-lice solution and the victim blaming.
Have you been playing with Gemma Mason, again?
Notorious nit-carrier. Of course I had.
Gemma had a sparkly pencil case
and smelled like Fruit Pastilles.

Head over basin, my mum would pour
that lemony petrol through my hair
and I would sit still for twelve whole minutes,
feel the crawling below the scalp come to an end,
wait for her to scrape the skeletons from my head
until it was mine again.

As an adult I don't know how many times
I have longed for nits. For their explicability,
their solution. A way to account for the crawling
below my scalp.

Oh God. How has this happened again?

I have dragged myself
to the bathroom, dry-mouthed,
with the bottle and the thirst for blame,
spent nights head over basin, pouring
petrol through my hair, praying for a spark
to rid this head that did not belong to me anymore.

Telling myself that forever is made up
of twelve minutes, over and over.
And if I sit still for long enough, twelve minutes
will bring a flame or flood or blade
to scrape the scuttling from my head,
until it is mine again.

LEARNING TO HOLD

There was once shit on the English block stairs.
Ashton said he could tell it was human.
Last week there was some in the library.

At school we only have urinals. If you need
to do what requires a cubicle to be done,
you must go to the nurse. And tell her.

Ask politely for the sticky key. Prise a bar of soap
and as much toilet paper as you estimate you will need
from her glare. *NOT the whole roll! I wasn't born yesterday.*

Hands full of wretched treasure, you must limp
through the crowds that laugh at you
until you reach the legendary room of cubicles.

Bolt the door behind you. Ignore the stench,
the muddy murals on the stalls,
stains swamping the floor.

Try not to question where they came from,
or inhale. Remember boys cannot be trusted
with themselves.

Hover. Do not touch what is not yours.
Flush. Do not leave a mess. Wash.
Do not make a scene. Remember.

It will take one trip, two at most,
for your body to learn itself locked,
to understand its release is conditional, inconvenient.
Humiliating.

One trip for you to recognise a boy's body
is a flooding sewer, engineered

to keep its outpour within,
swell on its own soil.
Retain.

Until the day
it can no longer bear to.

LION'S PRIDE

The logo on our blazers was a golden lion.
First ever assembly, our headteacher told us
we would grow from spotty cubs into full-maned
men, ready to seize the world at sixteen, ready
to take a mate from the girls' school next door.

Only one admitted to not wanting that.
He was reduced to carcass.
The smell of his blood
in the playground served as a warning:
this was not that kind of pride.

*

My body told itself this was right.
It is like convincing yourself you're a lion
when your ribs stripe your insides tiger.
Flamingo lining your lungs,
each breath in a chestful of shame.
Each breath out the red flag you are always
wiping from your lips, the scent of mealtime
you are forever washing from your skin.

*

When defending the weak from the teeth
of their hunters, teachers would say
why d'you keep bothering him?
do you fancy him?
are you gay?
Met by a classroom of hyena cackle.

Never more than the butt
of an accepted joke.
Not once, in five years, were the punchlines
embroidered into my chest
explained to me.

*

How we were taught to chew the word 'tolerance'
as if diversity were to be put up with,
as if diversity were the limp dog in the pack,
the lame bitch. How she is first to be turned on
when the heat is up.

*

My cousin told her teachers
that the jungle fight had become too hot,
that she could no longer outrun the howls of *DYKE*
which chased her down corridors.
She was told
you shouldn't have cut your hair so short.

*

Some nights the thought of what kind of animal
you might be was too much
to tame.

SUMMERTIME STRETCH

The year had moved slowly
so quickly as it always does.
Last we knew it was lying fat
on its face drunk on snow.
Now it had rolled over, sun
bathing topless on the park,
Kourtni's phone spitting Dizzee
Rascal. None of us could hear
the words, mainly just polyphonic
crackling. But we *felt* them.
Warmest summer on record.
We were what it made of us.
Night times, corner shop,
I'd put on Josh's
parka and he'd tell me
yeah, you well look eighteen.
Pineapple Bacardi Breezers
and a small bottle of clear
liquid that said
'vodka-flavoured spirit'.
Shotting metal mouthfuls
from the lid, swallowing
grimaces past wisdomless
jawlines. *yeah, tastes well good.*

did you hear what happened to Kayla?

Wet look hair gel
by the tub. Polo shirts,
collars up. Happy
slapping. Hoody
snatching.

yeah. Joe said he'd sell her the video
if she didn't show the police.

The smoke of Mayfair Menthol
Superkings sickening the evening
air, a month before Amy Winehouse

would sing us back to black blazers,
striped ties and discipline,
before we would learn
that the girls who did it
would not be suspended,
that the boys who filmed it
would not realise they had
done anything wrong,
that Kayla would not
return to school.
The year was rolling
onto its side again.
We were not sure whether
it was drunk or sick of us,
we just sat and listened
to the evening crackle.

WHEN SOMEONE HAS DROWNED

is it enough to say
it was the current that took her,
she was too far out to be saved?

Do our mouths not all drip
with the wetness
that dragged her?

Our hands
rip
tides?

LEARNING TO SWALLOW

Maisie would serve us doubles
and charge for singles after college.
If her supervisor was in earshot, she'd ask for ID
and we'd hand over our Nando's loyalty cards.
Vodka lemonades and cherry VKs, each week

I felt less red about being the only boy in the group.
We took turns choosing three tracks for £1 on the jukebox,
returning to the table, waiting for the look
on each other's faces when our songs dropped. TLC
and Craig David, singing along like we were in concert.

One week the football was on.
Two brickhouse-built men, with the tattooed fists
and chipped shoulders I knew too well,
stood at the bar and stared at me.
Knuckle-duster stared.

The girls didn't notice.
The table caught fire
and the glue holding up my forehead melted,
my teeth fell out and buried me
and the girls didn't notice.

Next round I ordered a pint of beer.
Maisie laughed. I went red.
She pulled me a half of cider,
which barked when I grabbed its neck.
I shouted at the screen to hide the noise.

I couldn't look them in the eye
when my next songs came on; Johnny Cash,
or something else my dad might have played.
The girls mocked the deep voices and mimed along,
I didn't have the words.

IATROGENIC

(adj.) describing illness or disease caused by the medical treatment of another condition

The doctors couldn't explain it.
Not a side effect of the drugs, they said.
I think it came from the plastic.

I watched a documentary about all the toxins
in plastic, what they can do to the body.
My dad spent hours on the oncology ward

each week, new chemical blood coursing
into him through clear plastic tubes.
He was on the most aggressive dose.

So strong, I think, it stripped something away
from the lining of those plastic canals
and washed it, cast away, into his body as well.

That must be what caused the adenoid otitis:
inflammation of the inner ear and throat tissue.
A minor complaint compared to everything else,

you wouldn't even diagnose it to look at him;
his neck appeared normal, still swallowed
and breathed as much as the tumours allowed.

His ears still understood the radio and my mother's
patience. It just meant there were some words
he couldn't get out. It meant there were certain

conversations he couldn't hear me start.
A stubbornness to the membrane.
Common in men of his condition, apparently,

but by nature impossible to treat.
It was not a problem, day to day,
but in the end it was the cruellest part.

TELLING THE LADS

but I'm not   like   a gay gay
you know   a vodka-cranberry gay
a here-and-queer gay
I'm more of just   like   a here gay
a steak and ale pie gay
an always think twice about whether
my shirt's a bit too gay gay
don't kiss in public
not a rub it in your face gay
no pink triangle stitched to conscience
wilted bouquet of police tape filling eye socket gay
I'm a hood up keep walking when *OI BATTYBOY*
slaps the back of your head type gay
a keep your mouth grateful gay
know your height gay
keep small keep polite gay
a sorry sorry sorry sorry sorry sorry sorry
for the audacity of a tongue gay
such inconvenient lungs
a turn on your own gay
a when they came for them gay
lips split not outspoken
a dying to unsleep myself awoken gay
a dying to be gay gay
you know   dying
just
to be
gay

DELIVERANCE

verbatim

I've known it from the day
he were born.

I were in the hospital
and the midwife put him on my chest
and I held him
and I felt him
you know, *felt* him

and I says to myself
I says
Joanne

this baby

is a gay

a gay baby.

And I just thought
well

that's that.

I love him
no different.

That's that.

We, born into sandpits silted
with the legacy of stolen milk
and forbidden storybooks.
Washcloth children,
wrung of any last drop of self
which catches the light,
soaked in the idea of manhood
spilled from the knuckles of our peers,
yet still they call us limp,
yet still with us they try
to wipe the floor.

> Mother in thy mercy,
> hear our prayer.

LANDSLIDE IN THE CHESTERFIELD AREA

Welcome to passengers joining us
here   at Leicester.   This is the delayed 2.40
       East Midlands Trains service   to Sheffield.
Apologies for the late running of this service. This is due to
        repair works following   a landslide
in the Chesterfield area   earlier this week. Once again
a landslide   in the Chesterfield area   earlier this week.
Delays were added to by a slow-running Cross Central service
ahead of us until Bedford today.
An at-seat service of light refreshments will commence shortly.
        Apologies again for the delays
caused by the landslide   in the Chesterfield area
    earlier this week.   The land slid
resulting in   a landslide.
Thank you.

'MAKE LEICESTER *BRITISH*'

They're talking about you, Leicester.
Saying you have too much curry sauce
on your fish and chips to taste like home.
Too many colours in your Union Jack
for it to be flown full mast,
saying you ain't British.

Tell them the truth.

Tell them how I only made Sheep #2 in our school nativity,
but I was cast as Rama in the Diwali play that year
and I was bloody great. Classmates of all faiths
gathered to celebrate acceptance of light.
How you raised hungry minds,
bellies full: tarka daal, jerk chicken, shepherd's pie.
School trips to churches, gurdwaras, mosques,
apart from the free food, all just buildings to us.
Tell them of the day that bus full of hate
rolled up on your doorstep,
the angry men, an organised pack:
a 'league of defence' which only seemed to attack.
Yet despite the wrath of those furious men,
an entire city stood united to face them.

Tell them, Leicester.

City who says it like it is.
Because they're twisting your turnstiles
into a picture which doesn't exist;
bandits, beggars and the bad in between.
Overwhelming our housing, flooding our GPs.
But you are the one to make them see, Leicester.
Because you work.
Your cobbled streets bow at the feet
of sari shops and bakeries holding hands,
masala fireworks sizzling bright, stretching out
to kiss the dales goodnight.

Tell them.

Because they have forgotten their history.
1915. 1940s. *Empire Windrush.*
London transport. NHS.
All the 'un-British' support
that saved them from their own mess.
Don't let us twist ourselves into a picture
which does not exist,
we who say it like it is.
Immigrants helped build this country.
Let fact be known.
If they are looking for someone to blame
for the new mess they are in,

tell them, look a little closer to home.

LANDSLIDE IN THE CHESTERFIELD AREA

Welcome to passengers joining us here at
     Derby.   This is the delayed 3.05 East Midlands Trains
service to   Sheffield.   Delays have been caused
by the Chesterfield area   sliding away
from the rest of the country   earlier this week.
Please report any sightings of it to a member of the on-board team.
      Do notify us of any suspicious behaviour you see
on our stations and trains as we do believe the incident may have been
caused   by terrorists.
Delays were added to by a slow-running Cross Central service today.
Once again Cross Central Trains
      are maliciously slow. Do not travel with them.
Thank you.

FROM THE MIDLANDS

Hi.
I'm the Midlands.
Thought I should re-introduce myself
because you never acknowledge me.
And I'm tired of being stuck
in between you two.

                                        The South.
                  Youngest child, getting all the attention.
          The one they could afford to put through private school.
                    Silver spoon fed your way up the food chain,
                        a clueless predator. *Not my fault I'm so perfect,*
                  looking down on us like we're not above you
                                                geographically.

The North.
Eldest child, has it the worst and don't we all know it.
Lining grudges along your knuckles like pints on a bar,
you have the wisdom to fill quarries but no one sees
past your work boots. Deep vowels and hard graft,
good enough for their call centres,
not for dinner with company,
apparently.

                        And then me: Midlands middle child.
                        Both of you pushing me into the other.
              South of Sheffield, doesn't mean I'm Southern.
                                  North of Potter's Bar
                          does not mean I am Northern.
                      I'm made up of twelve *real* counties.

I may not build ships,
may not have a Harrods
but I am the founder of pork pies.
And several brands of cheese.
I'm at the heart of this country; I start the mountains
up its spine, lead the train tracks
pumping its blood.

Thank you, by the way,
for the precious few platforms you spared for me, London.
And for the patronising blue footprints you painted
on the escalators leading to them.
We just wouldn't have known where to stand.
Your etiquette is so different to ours. Family tree unto yourself, forgot
the capital was planted in my neck of the woods
back in the day.

Forgot the roots that grew you,
now you have a monopoly on gentrification
like that's your middle name, charging Mayfair rent down Old Kent
Road like this is a game. But I don't play like that, London,
which is why your people commute back to my bed at night.
You need to learn how to keep yours
satisfied, London.

I'm the Midlands.
Bore the brains of Isaac Newton, the soul of Beverley Knight
and the rugged sexual appeal of David Attenborough.
Robbing the rich and feeding to the poor, I've got legends
in my forests and kings beneath my car parks,
got royalty running through my tarmac.

Forgotten sibling.
Might not look much to you,
might come out a bit rough on a Friday night
but I scrub up nice when I need to.
I'm diamond, duck. The strength
that stops you folding at the middle,
the beauty that makes this crown shine.

I am the Midlands.
Remember me.

WHEN THE STRANGER CALLED ME A FAGGOT

I did not blink

instead   this time   my mouth filled with
Grimsby's chip cone, wooden forks
and Aylestone Leisure Centre, rolling hills, walks to school,
my first cigarette bought off Josh Baker for 50p
and the taste of being short-changed and the taste of being told
it is fair, K-Swiss, The Old Horse, my overworked father,
uncles asking about girlfriends at Christmas, my cousin's knee,
my broken nose and the kitchen roll unable to soak up
a family's damage, funeral faces, graffiti
on the back of our livers and Churchgate, Maryland Chicken,
free entry before eleven, bottles tossed into dancing crowds,
lips greeting glass with crimson splutterings of *hallelujah,*
and fifth period French, savages born of boredom,
fighting Ashley down the science block, crowd of camera-phones
blocking us in, no way out for one
and Nickesh and Chris and Sam,
Mecca Bingo and wash brook, the boy who got snatched,
chewing gum sticking eyelashes together,
football practice and get it together lads,
my hand on his leg, shower room and eyes forward lads,
his hand in my mouth
and or what or what or what.

and my new friends said,
we haven't heard you like that before

and I said,
you haven't heard me.

LANDSLIDE IN THE CHESTERFIELD AREA

Welcome to passengers joining us here at
     the region formally known   as Chesterfield.
This 3.20 East Midlands Trains service to Sheffield is delayed
following the collapse   of the northern hemisphere
earlier this week.   Please note that Cross Central Trains
are shite.   They serve lukewarm tea and support terrorism.
     Would all passengers in the silent coach please
get over yourselves.
Thank you.

WHEN I SEE

a father
kiss his grown son,
my lips sink
and my heart lifts.

Tell us we are not the bite marks,
the dirt or scab.
It is not for us to lift ourselves
from the skin of this town.
We have the same right to walk its street,
kiss its sky without the crows' gossip,
without the wind churning with the need
to teach us a lesson or two.

Mother in thy mercy,
hear our prayer.

LEARNING TO DRIVE

The self-defence of Julie Gianni, Vanilla Sky

'I swallowed your cum. That means something.'

in other words

I am a person of stomach.
I do not un-clutch myself for just anyone.
Your body made me promises that felt safe enough
to drive along. You are the one who broke the guardrail.

in other words

Do you know how difficult it is pretending
to enjoy drinking beer? The bitter depth
of being your 'buddy' foaming the back
of my throat. I am bloated with you,
I eat breakfast and cannot unthink your hips,
and yet you force me to sit
in the bar with you and laugh,
as stories of other women
ooze over your chin and ferment in your lap.
You squeeze my thigh under the table,
invite me to your room, expect me to fold
over into your crash test dummy.
And I do.

in other words

Yes, I did Cameron Diaz my car off the bridge
with you in the passenger seat.
Yes, I made a love letter of your face
across the dashboard. But
you were the one who chose to get inside,
who fastened the seatbelt of his voice
into my ear and told me to let go.
You are the only man I have ever
closed my eyes behind the wheel for.

You are the one who left me
soaked into hotel room towels
alone
knowing full well that was not the deal
your body shook on.

in other words

Sorry
about the disfiguration and everything,
but all you ever gave me was face.
I am the one who died.

SUMMER JOB LIFEGUARDING ON LAKE FISHKILL

They told us we were the police of the water,
during training. We learned to raise bodies

from the waves with the most urgent delicacy.
How to spot a drowning child, how to profile them.

Two weeks into the summer, a girl
in the deepest part of the lake slipped

beneath the surface with barely a gasp of a goodbye.
It was the first time I'd felt the terror of my heart

choking on a beat. I pulled her from the depths
with no delicacy, just panic. But she was alive.

As news of this floated to the others, instead of relief,
a ripple of envy surfaced. Train a group of people

in emergency for long enough,
emergency they will long for.

Four more children went
under that summer.

All survived. Rescuers bathed in glory.
Rescued left wondering why

they had been encouraged
into the deep

when the guards knew
they could not swim.

NOTES FROM MYKONOS BEACH AT 3AM

On the other side of town, where graffiti and stray dogs rule,
a church sits on a cliff, waiting for the purple ribbon horizon
to pull up a new day, refusing to acknowledge the men
gathered in the shadows under its nose. The gentle sea

laps as if it doesn't know what they are doing, either.
Salty waves falling against rock face. Bodies swallowed
by darkness. Silhouettes standing, knelt. Writhing in worship.

I wonder which of these midnight disciples
have mortgages, or families back at their hotels.
How many wives are lying in resort bedrooms,

remembering the man who named each breast
on their honeymoon, dreaming
of a husband who can sleep at night.

NOTES FROM THE AIRPORT BAR,
A WEEK LATER, INTOXICATED

Draft 1.

i saw you through the chip-fat haze, mcdonald's in a foreign city.
we can all relate to a disgustingly low meat content drunken meal
after a few bevoirs. and there you were sitting on a stool, swivelling,
dreamy. i walked past you like i didn't even know you were there
oh oh (anyone who likes shania twain will get that). you made a
joke and i said *mmm.* you said *what?* and i didn't say anything, i
just laughed and a bit of chip came out of my nose. yes, i might be
drunk but you, my friend, are beautiful. and people won't believe
me tomorrow because they've crawled off like beetles to find dung
and strobe lights and i needed a break before to fill up for the
treat but found the dung. you are the dung! a big beautiful ball of
dung. *what's your name?* you asked and i told you and i waited three
seconds before asking you because i am disinterested and cool
and your name is marcus. marcus my mcdonald's man. you have a
face like a star. bright. biblical, your face led men to a messiah that
ended up being jesus. your face is religiously beautiful and i am
being aloof so i just keep looking at the door and not making eye
contact. the woman asked me what i wanted to eat and i said, *NO.*
take me home. but don't because i'm celibate and independent and
i'm pretty sure i know people in here. so i take your number and
your teeth are like clear bulbs hanging from a wire at a summer
barbecue, brightening the night. i mean they're not proportionally
like that, you don't have massive gap teeth. quite the opposite.
take me home. don't. i'm coy and aloof with my own OVEN. but
whatever, i don't give a shit, i have your number and you are
beautiful and i say goodbye and i leave and i text you something
bland and non-committal like 'hi, this is me. hope you got home ok.'
and you reply with something equal, 'you too. it was great to meet
you.' and i'm drunk and i don't give a shit: 'it was LOVELY to meet
you too x'

two days later i lose my phone, and you.

there are over 1,000 marcuses in this city.
none of their profile pictures resemble you.

at all.

where are you?

where are your light bulbs

and shine?

NOTES FROM THE SEXUAL HEALTH CLINIC WAITING ROOM

As I lay in your bed
looking at your eyes,
I knew deep inside,
at some point in the near future,
I would be weeing into a cup.

*

The room smells like anxiety and hair-removal cream.
Capital FM is playing power ballads
and I am trying not to touch anything,
including the air, which is silent
apart from an occasional cough and Meatloaf
letting us know he would do anything for love.

*

A teenager with his dad blushes into the corner.
Rachel Taylor had sex for the first time
when we were fifteen and she told her mum
and her mum kicked off and brought her here
and afterwards she took Rachel to Bella Italia for dinner
and Rachel said it was the closest they'd ever been.

*

Roses are red,
violets are blue,
if I have gonorrhoea,
you need to start a course of preventative antibiotics.

*

Why do I picture my nan looking at me
as if I were the badger
who ruins the church flowerbeds at night?

Wicked creature revelling in Godless
mischief, dark holes.
Still, something about
the confession,
the scraping from within,
the offering of blood,
makes me something sacred,
no?

*

Whoever invented
the 'no news is good news'
results delivery system
is a fucking
sociopath.

*

Divinity is all well and good on a Sunday morning
but what of a Friday night, or the slow unsheathing
of Wednesday afternoon, when the ache
for empty head and bent knees cannot be soothed
by prayer alone, when scripture cannot buy you a drink
and make you feel un-empty again?
Surely even God,
between the tangled sheets
of Her condemnation and forgiveness,
has, at least once,
weed into a cup.

SAMARITAN

The face of a man who looks like your father
hangs above a helpline number
down the far end of the platform.

Rain has soured the hopeful green lettering
across his face to mouldy purple.
We all feel desperate sometimes.
Speak soon. Talking helps.

You wonder how many delayed journeys
it took for them to decide these posters
were a sound investment, who wrote the copy,
how much the model was paid,

has he met himself in his darkest hour
and wished he never took the job?
His frown asks you why you're standing
so close to the tracks.

You ask his frown if it can climb inside you
like the other boys did to make you step back.
Can it undo you? Spoon out the mud,
make the shaft of the rail look less desirable?

It says, *no.*
You touch the model's printed lips.
He licks them, the way that your mother licked hers
the last time she kissed your father.

Savouring a taste
which would not return to the mouth.
He looks at the oncoming train
and back at you, closes his eyes.

He cannot bear to say goodbye,
same as your mother.
Speak soon.

GRAVE

A pair of his briefs lie grieving
at the bottom of my wash basket.
They have not moved in months.
Like me, they ask,

What is the use of us now he is gone?
The man who bought us new and broke us
in. Did we not do all he asked?
Hold the secret of him in our palm,
stitch our skin compliant around it?
Did we not stretch the seams of our self,
mould to fit him so perfectly
that we became not fit for another,
that even now we cannot tell
our skin from his
stink?

How does he still own us?

Why do we still wake buried
in the impossible dream
of him returning to put us on
one last time,
his skin still warm,
his sweat in our mouth
still sweet,
sickening?

WHEN YOU HOLD SOMETHING IN

for so long,
sometimes the only way
for it to come out
is through your blood.

THE BOY WHO PRAYED

i

A young boy, bringing together soft maps of innocence not yet
creased by this world, got on his knees and prayed. At the end he
said, *P.S. God, if you ever need someone to talk to, I am here.*

He did not know God would take him at his word. All of the things
God had on Her mind. Terrible things She had been longing to
get off Her chest. They flooded his head like locusts, boils, rivers
of blood: the eleventh plague had been waiting, filling his body
with false idol and sin, but no one could see why his face would
twitch and his limbs would shudder. They looked him in the eye
of the storm behind his forehead but could not see the turbulence
in his lungs, the lightning striking holes in his gut, stomach always
sinking.

When they heard of a sick child, they thought chicken pox,
not an affliction Calpol couldn't calm, plasters wouldn't cover.
They did not believe that a child, with so little in their brain,
could have so much on their mind.

ii

With blind eyes turned he carries on believing
these to be confessions from God. Her guilt builds his cabin pressure,
air sickness, he reaches for an oxygen mask which isn't there: a way
to breathe, to say stop, I'm sorry, I can't be your psychiatrist anymore,
God. Only room for one on this leather couch and I think I need
to lie down, think I'm feeling a bit poorly. You let yourself into my
mind but didn't shut the door behind you, I should have said this was
invite only but I didn't know you were friends with demons, God, I
didn't know the highwaymen you rode with who would hijack my
happiness and now I'm held hostage to a light switch
one two   switch on   one two   switch off   and people
just laugh at me, just point and laugh at the freak in the doorway,
flicking the switches and washing my hands and I want to scream *I
am doing this for you*, without my   one two   one two   the whole wide
world would switch off, the weight of the whole wide world is on my
back but I've nothing in my hands but these maps that won't tell me
where to go. I am lost, God.

iii

If I could speak to him now, I would say, young boy,
you are doing so well. I know what they don't;
I know your shoulders make London Bridge look like Lego
with the loads they bear. I know you start each day talking the
voices in your head down from ledges.
I know where you bleed.
I know why.
Brave boy,
this too shall pass.

LEARNING TO DANCE

We carried on with our day as planned. Hungover in the heat, beach with '90s music shimmying from speakers, as it had done the night before, when we danced in the club where men held hands, unchallenged. We went to dinner that night young and alive. An American woman on the next table broke more of the story than the morning headline could bear to: fifty dead, gay nightclub, homophobic attack. M a y b e .

The conversation then continued, as a wake or afterlife might. The words moving on so easily, my throat swelled. Eyes tidal. I could not hold back the break of this wave. I sat in my chair and cried into my food, into the broth, the vessel, the earth. I was very aware of how terribly un-British this was.

And	And	And	And
I had met	this was	such	selective
none	not a	terrible	mourning
of these	story	things	is a boat
people.	about	happen	capsized
	me.	every	by the weight
		day.	of its own
			hypocrisy.

And yet I couldn't not cry. I could not stop. I thought of my hometown, the two men set on fire outside of the bar where they had once held hands unchallenged.

I feel a dance floor clutching her womb and falling. I feel them. Daughter, brother. Lover who had shared my bed, who likely knew even more than I of what hatred looked like in its various Sunday suits: fist, lighter fluid, politician, estranged parent. Who all likely knew the fight and were on a cigarette break from it because Saturday night had arrived, her speakers shimmying, her flawless black sequin thighs grinding us up a new moon to worship.

And they just wanted to dance.

In the name of Jonathan, David
and the brothers we have wept for.
In the name of all the siblings
we lost along the way,
whose cries were not listened to in time,
whose hands sung their own eulogy,
whose bodies crochet us a better
sky to dream under,

        Mother,
        hear.

ACCORDING TO THE BOOK OF SAMUEL

a cento, interrupted

David said unto Jonathan
I have found grace in your eyes.

> *And did he not find himself in mine?*

Jonathan stripped himself of the robe
that was upon him and gave it to David,
said whatsoever thy soul desireth
I will do it for thee.

> *And did my tongue not strip itself of the bricks*
> *that were upon it for him? Did he not take them*
> *and build me a baptism?*

Jonathan delighted much in David
because he loved him.

> *And later, did I not delight inside of him*
> *much? Did I not keep a shrine*
> *of his robes in my wardrobe?*

It came to pass that the soul of Jonathan
was knit with the soul of David
and he loved him as his own soul.

> *And later, was he not as much a part of me*
> *as anything had ever been? Did I not recognise in him*
> *the empty of my soul, and see in myself the fullness of his?*

And when Saul sent his messengers
to take David, Jonathan fell on his face
to the ground and they kissed one another
and wept one with another until David exceeded.

> And when I was forced to flee, did we not weep
> and kiss and bow our backs
> in plea for another way?

And Jonathan was slain, was fallen by the sword,
and David mourned and wept and fasted,
David lamented over him,
Thy love to me was wonderful.
How the mighty are fallen.

> And when we realised we had fallen by the sword
> did I not go hungry and blue for him?
> Do I not still? Is a shrine of him
> not inside me now?

NOTES

Prayers combine to form the poem *Prayers for the battyboys of LE2*, shortlisted for the Outspoken Prize for Poetry 2017. Individual prayers received two High Commendations in the Her Heart Poetry Awards 2017.

Grandpa Terry was shortlisted for the York Literature Festival/ Yorkmix Poetry Prize 2017 and awarded a Commendation.

From the Midlands was long-listed for the Outspoken Prize for Poetry 2016.

When the stranger called me a faggot won the Silver Wyvern Award and first prize in the Poetry on the Lake 2017 poetry competition main category, judged by Carol Ann Duffy.

Learning to drive won Honorary Commendation in the Café Writers Poetry Prizes 2017, judged by Andrew McMillan.

Iatrogenic is after Caroline Bird's, *Mystery Tears*.

'a cento, interrupted' of *According to the Book of Samuel* is after Andrew McMillan's, *Saturday night: a broken cento for Thom Gunn*.

ACKNOWLEDGEMENTS

My thanks to the editors and staff at the following publications and websites where earlier versions of these poems appeared, sometimes under different titles:

Harvests of New Millennium, Homing Pigeon, Magma, Next Generation Speaks Anthology, Orbis, Out-Spoken, StAnza, THE ANNUAL 2017 (Her Heart poetry), *The Best Slam / Stand-up / Performance / Spoken Word Poetry Book in the World* (Burning Eye Books), *The Black Flamingo* zine (Tate Modern), *The Purple Breakfast Review, Yorkmix*.

This collection would not be possible without my incredible mother, who has always heard me, my formidable sister and my dearly missed father.

Thanks to the team at Burning Eye Books for your faith and patience. Big thanks to Maria Twinkletoes Ferguson, Alice Frecknall, Anna Freeman, Gabriel Jones, Vanessa Kisuule, Ian Mckewan and Gabby Peeters – your work as artists and your feedback at various stages of the process have guided me greatly. Thanks to Jennifer Militello for the workshops that helped birth some of these poems. Thanks to Kate and Harris for your input. Special thanks to Andrew McMillan – your work, your support and your guidance have been invaluable in shaping this book.

I would like to thank Korde Tuttle, G Yamazawa and Corpus Collective '13 for supporting me from the beginning and for continuing to be an inspiration, both on and off stage. James North for being the best supporter, critic, friend and diva I could ask for. Roz, Rach, Kourtni, Bonney and the rest of my beloved Leicester family, who all feature here under various guises. Thank you to everyone who has read this book and to those who have not.